101 TROPICAL DRINKS

Photography © 2013 by Alexandra Grablewski

Food styling by Brian Preston-Campbell

Prop styling by Martha Bernabe

For information about permission to reproduce selections from this book, write to Permissions, Houghton Mifflin Harcourt Publishing Company, 215 Park Avenue South, New York, New York 10003.

 www.hmhbooks.com

Library of Congress Cataloging-in-Publication Data

Haasarud, Kim.
 101 tropical drinks / Kim Haasarud ; photography by Alexandra Grablewski.
    1 online resource.
  Description based on print version record and CIP data provided by publisher; resource not viewed.

 ISBN 978-1-118-45675-0 (cloth : acid-free paper) -- ISBN 978-1-118-45680-4 (pdf) -- ISBN 978-1-118-45682-8 (epub) -- ISBN 978-1-118-45679-8 (mobi)
I. Drinks. I. Title. II. Title: One hundred one tropical drinks. III. Title: One hundred and one tropical drinks.
 TX951
 641.87'4--dc23
                                   2012035716

Printed in China

TOP 10 9 8 7 6 5 4 3 2 1

TROPICAL DRINKS

KIM HAASARUD

PHOTOGRAPHY BY ALEXANDRA GRABLEWSKI

HMH

HOUGHTON MIFFLIN HARCOURT
BOSTON NEW YORK 2013

INTRODUCTION

The tropical cocktail conjures exotic visions of swaying palm trees, white sandy beaches, gentle ocean breezes, and libations served from hollowed-out pineapples. Add to that the tastes of coconut, guava, ginger, and copious amounts of rum and you begin to get the picture. But lest we forget, tropical is a kindred spirit to tiki. And when we mention tiki, we have to pay homage to our founding fathers: Vic Bergeron of the legendary Trader Vic's and Don the Beachcomber.

Back in the 1940s, Americans were smitten with the lure of the South Pacific—it was exotic, it was adventurous, it was fun. C'mon, who wouldn't find shrunken heads, pirates, Hollywood icons frolicking in the sand, and fire-lit punchbowls exciting? It was just after the Depression and while most Americans couldn't afford to travel, they could indulge their thirst for adventure in some tiki cocktails. Back then, tiki cocktails were treasured proprietary drinks, with barmen guarding their recipes by writing them in code. They used many different rums, and concocted their own homemade syrups and liqueurs. Unfortunately, tiki cocktails suffered much like many of their classic cocktail brethren; fresh juices were replaced by bottled mixes, and classic rums were replaced by cheap impersonators. But now thanks to the tireless efforts of tiki historians and experts like Jeff "Beachbum" Berry, many of these original recipes have been rediscovered, and as a result the tiki movement is alive and well once again. Witness the opening in the past few years of great new tiki bars around the country, establishments like Smuggler's Cove in San Francisco; Forbidden Island in Alameda, California; and Painkiller NY and Lani Kai in New York City— just a few that would make Vic and Don proud.

In this book, I've included many classic tropical and tiki cocktails (thank you, Jeff Berry) as well as some reimagined ones. I've also taken liberty with some classic cocktails like the Cosmopolitan and Margarita and given them a contemporary tropical spin. Tropical and tiki drinks can run the gamut from super easy to make with a quick shake of a few ingredients to more involved productions requiring the layering of different rums, swizzling (see page 32), blending in a blender, making your own syrups, using bitters, infusing, and so on. In this introduction I've listed many different rums and their island characteristics, as well as liqueurs, other spirits, purees, bitters, juices, and more. But the whole point of a tiki drink is for it to be a little exotic with a whole lot of flavor—no stress.

So grab a good bottle of rum, flip through this book, and pick a drink that tickles your fancy and ignites your sense of adventure. Oh, and don't forget to raise a glass to the spirits of Vic and Don.

—Kim Haasarud

THE RUMS

Unlike any other spirit category, rums "play in the sandbox" really well. Meaning you can layer and mix them for added depth and flavor. While rums originated in the South Pacific (hence the reason they are so readily used in tropical and tiki drinks), they can be made anywhere in the world; the only restriction is that sugar cane is involved. The majority of rums are made from molasses, a by-product of making sugar. Others, however, are made straight from sugar cane juice. Below, I've listed rums by style and region to give you a better and bigger picture of how rums are made, classified, and characterized.

STYLES

WHITE/SILVER RUM. Usually clear. Most white and silver rums are aged, but are further distilled and filtered to remove the color. Great mixability.

GOLD/AMBER RUM. Light gold or amber. Usually aged for a few years. No regulation on how long it must be aged.

DARK RUM. Full bodied and darker in color. Quite a few are produced from pot stills and aged in oak. No regulation on how long it must be aged.

AGRICOLE RHUM. Appellation Controlee from Martinique, in the French West Indies. Made from distilled sugar cane juice. Light with a nice vegetal quality to it; buttery.

SPICED RUMS. A white, gold, or dark rum infused with spices and fruits.

FLAVORED RUMS. Rums (usually white rums) infused with flavors ranging from vanilla to coconut to mango.

ANEJO AND AGE-DATED RUMS. Blended aged rums. Age-dated rums, such as Bacardi 8, usually reflect the youngest aged rum in the blend.

RUM REGIONS

BARBADOS. Produces light and sweetish rums. One of the first regions that really started to put out a soft, smooth rum. Back in the eighteenth century, rum was well known as a fiery, almost unpalatable spirit. Barbados put rum on the map as a fine spirit. (George Washington actually requested a Barbados rum for his inauguration—that was the good stuff.) Current examples include Mount Gay and Foursquare.

CUBA. Light-bodied and crisp. One of the first regions yielding a very soft and smooth rum. Many rum connoisseurs associate Cuban rums (the predecessor to Puerto Rican rums) with being much like the rum version of a vodka: fairly neutral and smooth. Examples include Havana Club and Bacardi, established in Cuba, since moved to Puerto Rico.

DOMINICAN REPUBLIC. Full-bodied, aged rums from column stills. Examples include Ron Matusalem and Brugal.

GUYANA. Rich, heavy, Demerara rums aged for long periods of time (25 years), often blended with lighter rums. Examples include El Dorado.

HAITI. Full-bodied rums. Aged in oak casks three or more years. Examples include Rhum Barbancourt.

JAMAICA. Rich and aromatic. Some can be funky, wild, and rich and others soft and smooth. Examples include Myers, Appleton Estate, and Wray & Nephew.

MARTINIQUE. Contains the largest number of rum distilleries in the eastern Caribbean. Mostly agricole rhums. Often aged in French brandy casks three or more years. One significant factor about rums from this island is that they were awarded the prestigious French label *appellation d'origine controlee*, previously reserved only for wines and cheeses. Rums from this region can only be called *rhums*. Because the majority of these rhums are agricole, they are light, somewhat vegetal, and even buttery. Examples include Neisson Rhum Agricole.

PUERTO RICO. One of the biggest producers of rum. The white rums are known to be very smooth and even a somewhat neutral spirit. Very mixable. Examples include Bacardi, Ron de Barrilito, and Don Q.

TRINIDAD. Primarily light rums. Examples include 10 Cane and Angostura.

VIRGIN ISLANDS. Light mixing rums and flavored rums. Examples include Cruzan and a new tenant, Captain Morgan.

BRITISH VIRGIN ISLANDS. There is only one rum distillery left on these islands, one of the oldest in the world. Back in the seventeenth century, the British Royal Navy would make their own blend and ration it out to the Royal Navy officers. Examples include Pusser's.

GUATEMALA. Medium-bodied, aged rum. Examples include Ron Zacapa.

NICARAGUA. Medium-bodied. Examples include Flor de Cana.

VENEZUELA. Known for being rich. Some on the sweeter side. Examples include Ron Añejo Pampero and Santa Teresa.

BRAZIL. Mostly cachacas. Unaged. Examples include Leblon, Sagatiba, Boca Loca, and Cabana Cachaca.

UNITED STATES. Up and coming. Smaller, artisanal distilleries. Examples include Clearheart.

AUSTRALIA. Examples include Bundaberg.

OTHER "TROPICAL" INGREDIENTS AND SPIRITS

ALLSPICE DRAM. Aka Pimento Dram, flavored with allspice berries. This liqueur was only recently made available again in the United States, in 2008, under the name St. Elizabeth Allspice Dram. Very spicy; use in moderation.

LICOR 43. A bright yellow liqueur made from 43 aromatic herbs and spices including vanilla and citrus. The predominant flavor is vanilla.

MARASCHINO LIQUEUR (I.E., LUXARDO). Many assume that this liqueur will be sweet and taste like cherries. But it is actually made from the stems and pits of cherries, yielding a very earthy, wild, and funky flavor. It's quite delicious in cocktails, but use in moderation.

VELVET FALERNUM. A lime, clove, almond, and ginger liqueur. Used often in many tropical and tiki drinks.

ORANGE CURAÇAO VERSUS TRIPLE SEC. Both are orange liqueurs and can be interchanged. Orange Curaçao, however, is usually darker in color and has richer, more brandy-like flavors, whereas a triple sec is clear and has a more straightforward orange flavor.

BITTERS

Bitters are a must-have in many tropical drinks. They add a nice depth of flavor that mingles with all the ingredients. Bitters are alcohol-based (some are made from rum, brandy, or even Everclear, a grain alcohol) and heavily infused with aromatics, herbs, and botanicals. Just a dash or two is all you need. Nowadays there are over a hundred different bitters available, ranging from a classic bitters to orange to lavender to rhubarb to celery! You may be able to find some of the classic bitters such as Angostura or Fee Bros. at your local liquor or grocery store, but if you want to be more adventurous, check the following websites for a wide range of choices.

www.cocktailkingdom.com

http://the-bitter-truth.com

JUICES, PUREES, AND CREAMS

Many of the recipes included in this book call for tropical juices, purees, and nectars. Some of these can be found in the juice section of the grocery store or in the refrigerated section. If you are a fan of ultra-fresh juices, I recommend investing in a juice extractor to get the most flavor. A juice extractor will allow you to make your own juices, such as pineapple juice, ginger juice (to make your own ginger beer and ginger ale), watermelon juice, and grape juice.

There are also some great puree companies that harvest fruits at their ripest and flash freeze them, making for some pretty great purees. Perfect Puree of Napa Valley is a great one from California (order online at Amazon.com). Boiron is also a good puree company from France.

Some recipes also call for a coconut cream. Coco Lopez (found at most grocery stores) is your best bet.

SYRUPS

Following are some syrup recipes used throughout the book. As long as you keep them refrigerated, they should last for a couple of weeks. Some great syrup companies make some fine syrups if you wish to buy them instead. Monin sells an extensive array of syrups that can be purchased online at www.monin.com.

DEMERARA SYRUP. A 2:1 ratio of Demerara sugar to water. Demerara sugar is named after the colony of Demerara (Guyana) in South America where the sugar originally came from. The crystals are large, light brown, and can be hard to dissolve. I recommend heating this over a saucepan until the sugar dissolves, or simply blending up in a blender on low speed for about 20 seconds. Bottle and refrigerate.

FLEUR DE SEL SYRUP. This syrup actually involves making the Demerara syrup first (above). Combine 2 cups of Demerara syrup to 1 cup of fleur de sel salt. If the Demerara syrup is cold, heat in a saucepan over low heat and add the salt. Stir till dissolved. Bottle and refrigerate.

GRAPEFRUIT SPICED SYRUP. A mixture of 1 cup ruby red grapefruit juice (strained), 1 cup Demerara sugar, 2 dashes ground cinnamon, 2 whole cloves, and 1/8 teaspoon vanilla extract. Heat in a saucepan over low heat until sugar has dissolved. Remove from heat and let cool. Bottle and refrigerate.

GRENADINE. While you can find this at most grocery stores, nothing beats making this yourself. Combine a 1:1 ratio of white sugar to pomegranate juice. Heat over low heat in a saucepan to dissolve, or blend in a blender on low speed for 20 seconds. Bottle and refrigerate.

HONEY SYRUP. Combine honey and hot water in a 1:1 ratio. Stir until honey dissolves. Bottle and refrigerate.

LEMONGRASS SYRUP. Clean 3 stalks of lemongrass and chop. Combine the chopped lemongrass with 2 cups of sugar and 3 cups of water in a saucepan. Bring to a boil. Reduce to low and let simmer for about 10 minutes. (The mixture should reduce.) Let cool. Strain. Bottle and refrigerate.

ORGEAT SYRUP

Orgeat is a syrup made from almonds and used in many classic tiki cocktails, the Mai Tai being the most popular. While you can buy an orgeat syrup at your grocery or liquor store or online (almond syrup at Monin.com), I found this great homemade recipe from Daniel Shoemaker of the Teardrop Lounge in Portland, Oregon, via *Imbibe* magazine. Many thanks to them for allowing me to reprint it.

INGREDIENTS

   2¼ cups raw sliced almonds
   3½ cups water
   3½ cups distilled water
   3½ cups organic cane sugar
   1 ounce vodka
   ¼ tsp orange blossom water, or to taste

TOOLS

   Medium-sized stainless steel or glass mixing bowl
   Strainer
   Food processor, blender, or rolling pin
   Long-handled spoon
   1-liter glass jar or bottle, with lid
   Cheesecloth

Place the sliced almonds in the mixing bowl. Cover with water and let sit for 30 minutes. Strain and discard the water.

In a food processor or blender, lightly pulse the almonds until they are coarsely ground. (You can also do this with a rolling pin.)

Return the ground almonds to the bowl, cover with the distilled water, and soak for 4 to 5 hours, stirring the mixture well with the long-handed spoon every hour or so. Strain liquid into a 1-liter glass jar through a cheesecloth-lined strainer, pressing to extract as much as possible. Discard the almonds.

Add the sugar to the liquid, close the lid tightly, and shake the jar vigorously, repeating several times over 15 minutes, or until the sugar dissolves. Add the vodka and orange blossom water and stir thoroughly. Cover and store in the refrigerator for up to 2 weeks.

MAKES 2 TO 3 CUPS OF SYRUP

PASSION FRUIT SYRUP. In a saucepan, mix together 1 cup water, 1 cup sugar, and ½ cup of passion fruit puree (or a high-quality passion fruit nectar). Stir over low heat until the sugar is dissolved. Bottle and refrigerate.

PINEAPPLE SYRUP (REQUIRES JUICE EXTRACTOR). Remove the outer layer of a medium-sized pineapple. Juice the fruit in a juice extractor. Strain. Mix in a 1:1 ratio of pineapple juice to white sugar. Stir well. Bottle and refrigerate.

SIMPLE SYRUP. A 1:1 ratio of white sugar and water. For a single recipe, 1 cup of sugar to 1 cup of water should suffice. This can be made by simply mixing the two in a pitcher until the sugar dissolves or by heating in a saucepan. (Heating it will also make it a little thicker.) Bottle and refrigerate.

(RICH) SIMPLE SYRUP. Same as above, but use a 2:1 ratio of white sugar and water. Bottle and refrigerate.

SPICED PLANTAIN SYRUP. Slice a ripe plantain into ¼-inch slices and place in a saucepan. Add 3 cups water and 2 cups Demerara sugar. Add 2 dashes ground cinnamon, 3 whole cloves, and ¼ teaspoon vanilla extract. Heat over low heat until sugar has dissolved and it has started to boil, about 10 minutes. The plantains should be soft and the mixture reduced. Remove from the heat and let cool. Strain. Bottle and refrigerate.

SPICED SYRUP. Same as above, but without the plantain. Feel free to add more spices such as a few allspice berries, a star anise, some black peppercorns, and 1 or 2 strips of orange zest.

SUGAR-FREE SYRUP. For a lower-calorie drink, use a zero-calorie simple syrup made with Splenda. While you can make this on your own, I would highly recommend buying it from Monin.com. They have several zero-calorie syrups on the market, such as regular, blackberry, and triple sec flavor.

(1) MAI TAI

Probably the most famous of all tiki–tropical drinks. The classic is a very simple and delicious drink, created by Vic Bergeron of Trader Vic's in 1944 in Oakland, California. The story goes that Vic created this rum drink for some friends who were visiting from Tahiti. Upon tasting it, one of his friends exclaimed, "Maita'i roa ae!" which means "Very good of the very best!" Thus Vic named the drink the Mai Tai. Unfortunately, many restaurants and bars across the country have taken a number of liberties with the recipe, making drinks that are pale replicas of the original.

1 ounce silver or gold rum
¾ ounce fresh lime juice
½ ounce aged rum
½ ounce orange Curaçao or premium triple sec
½ ounce orgeat (almond) syrup (see page 14)
¼ ounce simple syrup (see page 15)
Float of dark Jamaican rum (optional)
Mint sprig, for garnish

Combine the silver or gold rum, lime juice, aged rum, orange liqueur, almond syrup, and simple syrup in a cocktail shaker. Top with ice and shake vigorously. Strain into a rocks glass filled with fresh crushed ice. Float the Jamaican rum on top, if desired. Garnish with the mint sprig.

(2) PLANTER'S PUNCH

great classic tropical punch. Quite a few variations of this cocktail exist on the Internet.

2 ounces dark rum
1½ ounces fresh orange juice
1½ ounces pineapple juice
½ ounce fresh lime juice
½ ounce simple syrup (see page 15)
Splash of grenadine (see page 13)
Dash of orange bitters (see page 11)
Maraschino cherry, pineapple leaf, and orange wheel, for garnish

Combine all the ingredients in a cocktail shaker. Top with ice and shake vigorously. Strain into a tall glass filled with fresh ice. Garnish with the cherry, pineapple leaf, and orange wheel.

(3) BLUE HAWAIIAN

One of the few vodka-based tiki drinks.

2 ounces pineapple juice
1 ½ ounces vodka
¾ ounce blue Curaçao liqueur
½ ounce fresh lime juice
½ ounce simple syrup (see page 15)
Splash of half-and-half
Pineapple leaf and lime wheel, for garnish

Combine all the ingredients in a cocktail shaker. Top with ice and shake vigorously. Strain into a tall glass filled with fresh crushed ice. (Or simply combine everything in a blender cup. Add ¾ cup of crushed ice and flash blend for 5 seconds. Pour into cocktail glass.) Garnish with the pineapple leaf and lime wheel.

(4) SIDEWINDER'S **FANG**

From the Lanai restaurant in San Mateo, California, circa 1960s.

1½ ounces fresh lime juice
1½ ounces passion fruit syrup (see page 15)
1½ ounces fresh orange juice
1 ounce Demerara rum
1 ounce dark Jamaican rum
3 ounces club soda
Long orange twist, for garnish

Combine the lime juice, passion fruit syrup, orange juice, and both rums in a blender with ½ cup of crushed ice. Blend for 10 seconds. Pour into a tiki mug or cocktail glass. Top with club soda and stir. Garnish with the orange twist.

(5) RUM RUNNER

Created in the early 1970s in the Holiday Isle Resort in the Florida Keys. Originally, the bartender concocted this recipe using leftover ingredients at the end of the night, but it soon became a hit. The name Rum Runner refers to rum smugglers during Prohibition. This is my version of the classic.

1½ ounces silver rum
1 ounce fresh lime juice
½ ounce blackberry liqueur
½ ounce crème de banana
½ ounce grenadine (see page 13)
½ ounce simple syrup (see page 15)
½ ripe banana, peeled, plus 2 slices for garnish
6 ripe blackberries, plus 2 for garnish

Combine all the ingredients in a blender cup. Blend for 10 seconds. Add ½ cup of ice and blend until smooth. Pour into a cocktail glass. Garnish with 2 blackberries and 2 banana slices.

(6) BAHAMA MAMA

2 ounces unsweetened pineapple juice
2 ounces fresh orange juice
¾ ounce silver rum
¾ ounce aged rum
¾ ounce coconut rum
½ ounce coconut cream (such as Coco Lopez)
½ ounce grenadine (see page 13)
Dash of bitters (see page 11)
½ ounce dark rum
Maraschino cherry, for garnish

Combine the pineapple juice, orange juice, silver rum, aged rum, coconut rum, coconut cream, grenadine, and bitters in a cocktail shaker. Top with ice and shake vigorously. Strain into a tall glass filled with fresh ice. Float the dark rum on top. Garnish with the cherry.

← (7) CARIBBEAN COSMOPOLITAN

1½ ounces Cruzan Mango rum
1 ounce white cranberry juice
¾ ounce triple sec
Splash of pineapple juice
Lime wedge
Pineapple stick, for garnish

Combine all the ingredients in a cocktail shaker. Squeeze in the lime wedge and discard. Top with ice and shake vigorously. Strain into a chilled cocktail glass. Garnish with the pineapple stick on the edge of the glass.

(8) GINGER BEER
(NON-ALCOHOLIC)

Ginger beer is similar to ginger ale, but much more intense. It's a common ingredient used in many tropical and tiki drinks. There are many on the market these days—many more than just a couple of years ago, including Reed's, Bundaberg, Gosling's, and one of my favorites, Fever-Tree. Most grocery stores carry them. But if you have the time (and a juice extractor), nothing beats making your own ginger beer. It's well worth the effort.

One of the best recipes I have found (and use frequently) is by Jeffrey Morgenthaler, a mixologist, blogger, and friend based in Portland, Oregon. Check out his website for some really juicy mixology tips: www.jeffreymorgenthaler.com. He has a few recipes, but this is one of my favorites because it's so dang easy. You start by making a "Ginger Syrup," which you can keep in the fridge for several weeks. Simply mix it with club soda when ready to serve.

4 parts club soda
3 parts Ginger Syrup (recipe below)

Mix the two over ice and *voilà!*

GINGER SYRUP

3 parts simple syrup (see page 15)
2 parts fresh lemon juice, strained
1 part fresh ginger juice (requires a juice extractor)

Combine all the ingredients in a pitcher or sealed container. Keep refrigerated until ready to use. Stir the mixture well prior to using.

A NOTE ON GINGER BEER. Ginger is a stomach settler and helps with nausea, so Ginger Beer (or a cocktail with Ginger Beer) is great to have on a boat, where seasickness often strikes. I've made these many times going back and forth from Marina del Rey to Catalina Island, where my husband and I used to live on a sailboat. It was our house cocktail.

(9) DARK & STORMY

One of the very few cocktails where a brand has actually succeeded in trademarking a cocktail (sort of). Technically, you can't call it a "Dark & Stormy" if you don't use Gosling's Black Seal rum, but, in all honesty, there are really only a few other rums on the market that could even come close to duplicating the same flavor. Most bartenders just add the rum with ginger beer. But, unless I'm making the ginger beer myself (see prior recipe), I like to add a little lime or lemon juice.

1½ ounces Gosling's Black Seal rum
½ ounce fresh lime juice
½ ounce simple syrup (see page 15)
4 ounces ginger beer (such as Gosling's Ginger Beer or Fever-Tree)
Mint sprig, for garnish

Combine the rum, lime juice, and simple syrup in a cocktail shaker. Top with ice and shake vigorously. Strain into a tall glass filled with fresh ice. Top with ginger beer and stir well. Garnish with mint sprig.

VARIATION: If you do make your own Ginger Beer, this is how I like to make my Dark & Stormy:

1½ ounces Gosling's Black Seal rum
2½ ounces Ginger Syrup (see previous page)
3 ounces club soda
Mint sprig, for garnish

Fill a tall glass with fresh ice. Add the rum. Add the ginger syrup. Top with club soda. Stir and garnish with the mint sprig.

(10) EL DIABLO

1½ ounces reposado tequila
3 ounces Ginger Beer, approximately (see page 26)
¾ ounce crème de cassis (or PAMA pomegranate liqueur)
Lime wedge

Fill a tall glass with fresh ice. Add the tequila. Add the ginger beer. Top with the crème de cassis. Serve with the lime wedge.

(11) MAJOR BAILEY→

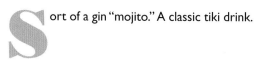

Sort of a gin "mojito." A classic tiki drink.

5 to 8 mint leaves
1 ounce simple syrup (see page 15)
½ ounce fresh lemon juice
½ ounce fresh lime juice
2 ounces gin (Plymouth is a good choice)
Lemon wheel
Lime wheel

In a Collins glass, muddle the mint leaves with the simple syrup, lemon juice, and lime juice. Add the gin. Top with fresh crushed ice and stir well. Garnish with the lemon and lime wheels.

(12) ZOMBIE

The story goes that Don the Beachcomber created this cocktail to help one of his hung-over customers get through a business meeting. He came back the next day and said that the drink had turned him into a "Zombie" for the entire day.

If you do an Internet search on the Zombie cocktail recipe, you are guaranteed to come across at least five versions and then some. But the one common factor in all of them is that they are made with a variety of different rums, including an overproof rum. All are strong and deadly, hence the name.

> 1 ounce dark or aged rum
> 1 ounce gold rum
> 1 ounce pineapple juice
> 1 ounce fresh orange juice (substitute another tropical
>   juice like papaya, passion fruit, or mango, if desired)
> 1 ounce fresh lime juice
> ½ ounce white rum
> ½ ounce apricot brandy
> ½ ounce simple syrup (see page 15)
> Float of overproof rum
> Maraschino cherry and pineapple wedge, for garnish

Combine the dark rum, gold rum, juices, white rum, brandy, and simple syrup in a cocktail shaker. Top with ice and shake vigorously. Strain into a tall glass filled with fresh crushed ice. Float of overproof rum on top. Garnish with the cherry and the pineapple wedge.

(13) DEMERARA DRY FLOAT

Another classic from Don the Beachcomber. This is my own delicious variation that is a little lighter on the citrus component.

2 ounces fresh lime juice
1½ ounces passion fruit syrup (see page 15)
1½ ounces Demerara rum
½ ounce simple syrup (see page 15)
¼ ounce maraschino liqueur (see page 10)
Float of overproof rum
Passion fruit, for garnish (optional)

Combine the lime juice, passion fruit syrup, Demerara rum, simple syrup, and maraschino liqueur in a cocktail shaker. Top with ice and shake vigorously. Strain into a tall glass filled with fresh crushed ice. Float the overproof rum on top. If fresh passion fruit is in season, garnish with a half a passion fruit. If fresh passion fruit is not available, omit the garnish.

(14) RUM SWIZZLE

The grandfather of all swizzle drinks. "Swizzle" is really the name of the tool used in making the drink. The original swizzle stick was a small dried branch found from a tree in the Caribbean islands that has a few extended smaller branches on the end that help to stir (or "swizzle") the drink. CocktailKingdom.com sells some great authentic swizzle sticks.

In making a Swizzle drink you need:

a) a swizzle stick (if you don't have one, the smallest hand-whip you can find will work)

b) a tall, skinny glass

c) fresh crushed ice

> 2 ounces rum (you can use a white rum, but I like the complexity of a slightly darker rum such as 10 Cane or even Cruzan Single Barrel)
> 1 ounce fresh lime juice
> 1 ounce simple syrup (see page 15)
> 3 dashes Angostura bitters
> Mint sprig, for garnish

Combine the rum, lime juice, and simple syrup in a tall glass. Top with crushed ice. Carefully push down the swizzle stick in the glass all the way to the bottom. Place the swizzle stick handle between the palms of your hands and rub together swiftly. (Use the same movement as you would when rubbing your cold hands to generate some heat.) This chills the drink very fast, mixes the ingredients, and lightly aerates them. When the drink develops frost on the outside of the glass (about 45 seconds to 1 minute), you know it's ready! Add the bitters right before serving. Garnish with the mint sprig.

(15) APEROL ABOUT IT

A group of us from Arizona Cocktail Week produced a pop-up tiki bar in town called the Tiki Hideaway. One of the drinks we served was called "Aperol About It," created by master mixologist and friend Jason Asher. This is a variation of the 1956 tiki cocktail the Demerara Sour using Aperol, an Italian aperitif. It's easy to make and soooooo good!

    2 ounces Appleton V/X (Jamaican) rum
    ¾ ounce passion fruit syrup (see page 15)
    ¾ ounce fresh lime juice
    ½ ounce Aperol

Combine all the ingredients in a cocktail shaker. Top with ice and shake vigorously. Strain into a rocks glass filled with fresh ice. (If you can use larger square cubes, those are ideal.) This drink has no garnish.

(16) EUREKA PUNCH

Created by Martin Cate, owner and creator of Smuggler's Cove in San Francisco. (If you've never been to this tiki bar, it's one of the best in the nation.) This cocktail is made with Yellow Chartreuse, an herbal liqueur created by the Carthusian monks in France. It's been around since the 1700s and is similar to the Italian herbal liqueurs Galliano and Strega. While probably not available at your local convenience market, you can surely find it at specialty grocery stores and online. They also make the more popular Green Chartreuse, which is more pungent.

> 1½ ounces fresh lemon juice
> 1½ ounces light-bodied amber rum (see page 7)
> 1 ounce honey syrup (see page 13)
> ½ ounce Yellow Chartreuse
> 1 dash of Angostura bitters
> 2 ounces ginger ale
> Lemon wedge or twist and mint sprig, for garnish

Combine the lemon juice, rum, honey syrup, Chartreuse, and bitters in a cocktail shaker. Top with ice and shake vigorously. Strain into a Collins glass filled with fresh ice. Top with ginger ale and stir. Garnish with the lemon wedge or twist and the mint sprig.

(17) GUAVA BASIL COOLER

Guava is such a great tropical flavor—it's tart, aromatic, and sweet all at the same time. It has a very short season and may be hard to find fresh. This cocktail uses a guava nectar you can usually find at most grocery stores. But if you do find fresh guava, by all means use it. I would flash-blend a small scoop of the fresh fruit in a blender with all the other ingredients and just a few cubes of ice.

I find that tequila goes really well with guava. The agave flavor plays nicely with the sweetness and tartness of the fruit.

> 1½ ounces reposado tequila
> 1½ ounces guava nectar (such as Kern's)
> 1½ ounces ruby red grapefruit juice
> ½ ounce St. Germain Elderflower liqueur
> ½ ounce fresh lime juice
> ½ ounce simple syrup (see page 15)
> 1 basil leaf, plus 1 leaf for garnish

Combine all the ingredients in a cocktail shaker. Top with ice and shake vigorously. Pour contents into a tall Collins glass. Top with additional ice, if needed. Garnish with a basil leaf.

(18) MANGO MAI TAI

A riff on the classic Mai Tai made with Cruzan Mango rum and a touch of mango nectar.

1½ ounces Cruzan Mango rum
1 ounce fresh lime juice
½ ounce aged rum (such as **Cruzan Single Barrel Estate rum**)
½ ounce orange Curaçao or triple sec
½ ounce simple syrup (see page 15)
½ ounce orgeat (almond) syrup (see page 14)
½ ounce mango nectar
Orange twist, for garnish

Combine all the ingredients in a cocktail shaker. Top with ice and shake vigorously. Strain into a tall glass filled with fresh ice. Garnish with the orange twist.

(19) FOG CUTTER

A classic tiki cocktail using gin and a sweet sherry.

2 ounces fresh orange juice
1½ ounces silver rum
1 ounce fresh lemon juice
½ ounce brandy
½ ounce gin
½ ounce orgeat (almond) syrup (see page 14)
¼ ounce sherry
Lemon wedge and mint sprig, for garnish

Combine the orange juice, rum, lemon juice, brandy, gin, and almond syrup in a cocktail shaker. Top with ice and shake vigorously. Strain into a tall glass filled with fresh ice. Float the sherry on top. Garnish with the lemon wedge and mint sprig.

(20) MORNING DEW SPARKLE →

½ ounce pineapple juice
¾ ounce Midori melon liqueur
2 ounces Moscato sparkling wine
Pineapple wedge, for garnish (optional)

Combine the pineapple juice and Midori in a cocktail shaker. Top with ice and shake moderately. Strain into a champagne flute. Top with chilled Moscato. Garnish with the pineapple wedge, if desired.

(21) CLASSIC DAIQUIRI

This is the traditional recipe, created in Cuba, simple, tart, and delicious. This is another cocktail that has really gotten its share of manipulation through the years.

2 ounces white rum
1 ounce fresh lime juice
1 ounce simple syrup (see page 15)
Thinly sliced lime wheel, for garnish

Combine all the ingredients in a cocktail shaker. Top with ice and shake vigorously. Strain into a chilled cocktail glass. Garnish with a floating lime wheel.

← (22) BANANA DAIQUIRI

So, now that we have the classic Daiquiri covered, this is a fruity twist on the original.

2 ounces aged rum
1 ounce fresh lime juice
1 ounce Demerara syrup (see page 12)
½ ounce crème de banana liqueur
½ ripe banana, peeled
Dried banana chip, for garnish (optional)

Combine all the ingredients in a blender cup *without* ice. Blend on High for 10 seconds. Add ½ cup of ice (preferably crushed). Blend on High for another 10 seconds. Pour into a cocktail glass. Garnish with a dried banana chip, if desired.

(23) HEMINGWAY
DAIQUIRI

reated by a bartender at the La Florida Bar in Cuba for Ernest Hemingway—who didn't like his drinks too sweet—this drink is also nicknamed "La Papa Double" because he was known to order "doubles."

There are quite a few variations of this cocktail, but this one is mine. I simply love this drink and it will always be one of my favorites. It was one of the first "real" cocktails I had when I lived in New York City and it still reminds me of what a great cocktail should be: layers of flavor, balanced, but not overly complicated.

I ounce light rum (such as 10 Cane rum)
¾ ounce fresh lime juice
¾ ounce simple syrup (see page 15)
¾ ounce fresh grapefruit juice
½ ounce dark rum (such as Zacapa 23 rum)
½ ounce Luxardo Maraschino liqueur (see page 10)
Dash of bitters (see page 11)
Grapefruit twist for garnish

Combine all the ingredients in a cocktail shaker. Top with ice and shake vigorously. Strain into a chilled cocktail glass. Garnish with the grapefruit twist or "flamed" grapefruit peel.

(24) PINEAPPLE NEEDLE

This is a great cocktail to make with an easy infusion. Pineapple is one of the best and easiest ingredients to infuse with alcohol because: a) it's available everywhere, b) it's relatively inexpensive, c) its soft flesh makes the infusion process happen very quickly, and d) it lasts for quite some time in the jar, unlike other fruits such as berries, which turn and change color rather quickly.

> **3 ounces Pineapple Infusion (recipe below)**
> **Pineapple wedge, for garnish**

Place the pineapple infusion in a cocktail shaker. Top with ice and shake vigorously. Strain into a chilled cocktail glass. Garnish with the pineapple wedge.

PINEAPPLE INFUSION

> **2 pineapples (or more as needed, depending on size of infusion jar)**
> **1 infusion jar**
> **1 liter premium vodka**
> **1 liter vanilla vodka**
> **1 liter coconut vodka or rum**
> **Optional: 2 vanilla beans, sliced open lengthwise**

Cut off the skin of the pineapple so that slices will be a hexagon shape. Cut off the flower top. Lay the pineapple on its side and slice into ³⁄₄-inch slices. Place them crisscross in the infusion jar, all the way up. Fill the infusion jar one-third with premium vodka, one-third with vanilla vodka, and the last third with coconut vodka or rum. Let stand overnight in a cool, dark place. Agitate the infusion and taste-test the following day. The longer the pineapple stays in the infusion jar, the sweeter it gets, but I don't recommend keeping it in the jar for more than 2 days. Strain the mixture and bottle. No need to refrigerate, since the alcohol acts as a preservative.

(25) BLACKBERRY PINEAPPLE
SIDECAR

A riff on the classic Sidecar, but with a tropical spin. Created by Ryan Magarian, bartender and proprietor of Oven and Shaker in Portland, Oregon.

7 ripe blackberries
1½ ounces fresh pineapple juice
½ ounce fresh lemon juice
½ ounce simple syrup (see page 15)
1½ ounces Hennessy VS cognac
½ ounce Cointreau
Pineapple leaf and/or lemon wedge, for garnish

In a mixing glass, muddle the blackberries with the pineapple juice, lemon juice, and simple syrup. Add the cognac and Cointreau. Top with ice and shake vigorously. Double strain into a chilled cocktail glass. Garnish with the pineapple leaf and/or lemon wedge.

(26) SUNBURN

I f you like "smokiness" in a cocktail, this one is for you. Mezcal is like the single-malt Scotch of the agave world: robust, earthy, and smoky. If the smoke element is too much for you, feel free to use tequila instead and maybe just a half ounce of mezcal.

5 mint leaves, plus sprig for garnish
3 orange wedges
¾ ounce fresh lime juice
½ ounce grenadine (see page 13)
½ ounce simple syrup (see page 15)
1½ ounces Del Maguey VIDA mezcal
Splash of club soda
Large orange peel or orange wheel, for garnish

In a mixing glass, muddle the mint leaves with the orange wedges, lime juice, grenadine, and simple syrup. Add the mezcal. Top with ice and shake vigorously. Strain into a tall Collins glass filled with fresh ice. Top with a splash of club soda and stir well. Garnish with the mint sprig and the orange peel or orange wheel along the inside of the glass.

(27) TROPICAL ITCH

Created in Hawaii in 1957 by Harry Yee, who was the first bartender to start putting paper umbrellas in his drink. Brought back to life by Jeff "Beachbum" Berry, this cocktail calls for an actual backscratcher as a garnish. You may take a nap after one of these, so a backscratcher comes in handy.

> 1½ ounces overproof rum
> 1 ounce dark Jamaican rum
> 1 ounce bourbon
> ½ ounce orange Curaçao
> 1 cup of passion fruit juice or nectar (such as Kern's)
> 2 dashes of bitters (see page 11)
> Pineapple stick and mint sprig, for garnish

Fill a large glass with crushed ice. Add all the ingredients. Using a swizzle stick (see page 32), swizzle together till completely frosted and mixed. Garnish with the pineapple stick, mint sprig, and a back-scratcher.

(28) PEGU CLUB
COCKTAIL

This cocktail hails from the city of Rangoon in Burma, near India, circa early 1900s.

2 ounces gin
¾ ounce Grand Marnier
½ ounce fresh lime juice
1 dash of Angostura bitters (see page 11)
1 dash of orange bitters (see page 11)
Lime wedge, for garnish

Combine all the ingredients in a cocktail shaker. Top with ice and shake *hard* for a good count to ten. Strain into a chilled cocktail glass. Garnish with the lime wedge.

(29) HURRICANE

Often associated with Mardi Gras, this classic from Pat O'Brien's on Bourbon Street has been bastardized to include powdered mixes and bottle drink mixes—a sickly sweet replica of the original recipe. Even the original bar has succumbed to using these mixes. The Hurricane glass was actually created after this cocktail by Mr. Pat O'Brien himself. While many variations still exist, this one is pretty close to the original. Note that if you've had this cocktail before at restaurants and bars around the country, it is usually red, which is due to a passion fruit syrup or Hurricane mix that is red in color. Real passion fruit juice and syrup is yellow-orange.

> 4 ounces dark Jamaican rum (or half light rum and half darker, aged rum)
> 2 ounces fresh lemon juice
> 2 ounces passion fruit syrup (see page 15)
> Maraschino cherry and lemon wedge, for garnish

Combine all the ingredients in a cocktail shaker. Top with ice and shake vigorously. Strain into a tall glass or a Hurricane glass. Top with crushed ice. Garnish with the cherry and a lemon wedge.

(30) GRILLED PINEAPPLE
MARGARITA

I grilled pineapple ring, cut in half (recipe below), plus I
    wedge for garnish
4 ounces reposado tequila
2 ounces agave nectar
I ounce premium orange liqueur
I ounce Licor 43 (see page 10)
I ounce fresh lime juice
I ounce fresh lemon juice

Combine all the ingredients in a blender cup *without* ice. Blend on
High for about 15 seconds. Add 1½ cups of ice (preferably crushed)
and blend on High for another 15 seconds. Pour contents into a
cooler glass. Garnish with the grilled pineapple wedge.

GRILLED PINEAPPLE

Slice a pineapple into ¾″-rings. Throw on a hot grill, just long
enough to make grill marks on both sides. Take off the heat. Cut
one of the slices into wedges, for garnishes. Cut the skin off the
other slices and use for the drink recipe above.

(31) BLACK PEPPER MANDARIN
MARGARITA

bright and fruity cocktail with a bit of black pepper heat.

3 to 4 orange wedges
1 ounce simple syrup (see page 15)
1 ounce fresh lime juice
¾ ounce silver tequila
¾ ounce Hangar One Mandarin Blossom vodka (or other orange vodka)
2–3 turns of freshly cracked black pepper

In a mixing glass, muddle the orange wedges with the simple syrup and lime juice. Add the tequila and vodka. Top with ice and shake vigorously. Strain into a Margarita glass and top with black pepper.

(32) TROPICAL MARGARITA

2 ounces reposado tequila
I ounce fresh lime juice
I ounce simple syrup (see page 15)
½ ounce Cruzan Mango rum
½ ounce triple sec
½ ounce fresh orange juice
¼ cup pineapple chunks
Pineapple leaf, pineapple wedge, and lime wedge, for garnish

Combine all the ingredients in a blender cup. Blend on High for 10 seconds *without* ice. Add ½ cup of ice (preferably crushed) and blend on High for another 10 seconds. Pour into a cooler glass. Garnish with the pineapple leaf, pineapple wedge, and lime wedge.

(33) CORONA-RITA

The ultimate in beach Margaritas, for the beer and tequila lover.

I½ ounces reposado tequila
I½ ounces simple syrup (see page 15)
I ounce fresh lime juice
¾ ounce triple sec
½ ounce fresh lemon juice
I Coronita (small bottle of Corona)

Combine the tequila, simple syrup, lime juice, triple sec, and lemon juice in a cocktail shaker. Top with ice and shake vigorously. Strain into a Margarita glass filled with fresh ice. Pop open a chilled Coronita (small bottle of Corona) and dump the whole bottle, upside down, into the Margarita. Do this fast so you can leave the whole bottle just sitting in the Margarita glass. You can choose to sip the Margarita or pull the bottle up and let it infuse into the cocktail.

(34) BEACHBUM'S OWN

 A new tiki classic created in 1999 by Jeff "Beachbum" Berry himself.

1½ ounces light Puerto Rican rum
1¼ ounces Demerara rum
¾ ounce Licor 43 (see page 10)
¾ ounce passion fruit puree (see page 15)
¾ ounce fresh orange juice
¾ ounce unsweetened pineapple juice
¾ ounce fresh lemon juice

Combine all the ingredients in a cocktail shaker. Fill with crushed ice and shake vigorously. Pour contents into a tiki mug or bucket glass.

(35) MOSQUITO BITE

1 ounce white rum
1 ounce aged rum
1 ounce spiced syrup (see page 13)
1 ounce fresh ruby red grapefruit juice
1 ounce unsweetened pineapple juice
¾ ounce fresh lemon juice
½ ounce Licor 43 (see page 10)
Maraschino cherry, for garnish

Combine all the ingredients in a cocktail shaker. Top with ice and shake vigorously. Strain into a Collins glass filled with fresh ice. Garnish with the cherry.

(36) DRAGON'S BREATH

Dragon fruit seems to be a flavor popping up in cocktails and spirits. Real dragon fruit is exotic looking, fairly expensive, and has a pretty subtle flavor—a cross between a pear and a strawberry. Both SKYY and Bacardi make a dragon fruit spirit, and either would work in this cocktail. This tropical, sweet-heat drink starts out sweet and ends with a slow burn in the back of the throat.

> 2 ripe strawberries, hulled and cut in half; leave one half for garnish
> 1 ounce fresh lemon juice
> 1 ounce simple syrup (see page 15), plus more if needed
> 2 ounces SKYY Dragon Fruit
> ⅛ teaspoon Sambal (a spicy chili paste)

In a mixing glass, muddle the strawberries with the lemon juice and simple syrup. Add the SKYY Dragon Fruit and Sambal. Top with ice and shake vigorously. Double-strain into a chilled cocktail glass. (Note: If the strawberries are not very sweet, add another ¼ ounce simple syrup.) Garnish with a half-strawberry.

(37) MAINSAIL

I ounce vanilla vodka or rum
I ounce fresh lime juice
I ounce simple syrup (see page 15)
½ ounce Cruzan Mango Rum
½ ounce blue Curaçao
½ ounce pineapple juice
Pineapple leaf, for garnish

Combine all the ingredients in a cocktail shaker. Top with ice and shake vigorously. Strain into a Collins glass filled with fresh ice. Garnish with the pineapple leaf.

(38) THE KINGSTON CLUB

Created by badass bar manager and mixologist Jeffrey Morgenthaler of Clyde Common in Portland, Oregon.

I ½ ounces Drambuie
I ½ ounces pineapple juice
¾ ounce fresh lime juice
I teaspoon Fernet-Branca
3 dashes Angostura bitters
I ounce club soda
Large orange peel, for garnish

Combine the Drambuie, pineapple juice, lime juice, Fernet-Branca, and bitters in a cocktail shaker. Top with ice and shake vigorously. Add the club soda. Strain into a Collins glass filled with fresh ice. Garnish with the orange peel.

(39) LIME IN DA COCONUT

Malibu Rum used to be the only coconut-flavored spirit on the market, but now there are many: coconut-flavored vodka (SKYY, Pearl, and Ciroc), other coconut rums (Cruzan and Parrot Bay), and even a coconut tequila (1800 Coconut). You could really use any of these in this cocktail.

> 1½ ounces coconut-flavored spirit (see suggestions above)
> 1 ounce fresh lime juice
> 1 ounce simple syrup (see page 15)
> 1 ounce coconut water
> Lime wheel, for garnish

Combine all the ingredients in a cocktail shaker. Shake moderately. Strain into a Collins glass filled with fresh ice. Garnish with the lime wheel and a straw.

(40) QUEENS PARK SWIZZLE

> 8 to 10 mint leaves, plus sprig for garnish
> ½ ounce fresh lime juice
> ½ ounce Demerara syrup (see page 12)
> 3 ounces Demerara rum
> 2 dashes bitters (see page 11)

In a Collins glass, muddle the mint leaves with the lime juice and Demerara syrup. Add the rum and bitters and top with crushed ice. Using a swizzle stick, swizzle together till completely frosted and mixed (see page 32). Garnish with the mint sprig.

(41) MISSIONARY'S DOWNFALL →

This is a riff off the classic, originally created by Don the Beachcomber, circa 1940s. It's a beautiful cocktail—kind of like you threw a Mojito along with some pineapple and peach brandy into a blender and *bam*—Missionary's Downfall.

10 to 15 mint leaves, plus sprig for garnish
½ cup fresh pineapple chunks
1 ounce white rum
¾ ounce fresh lime juice
¾ ounce simple syrup (see page 15)
½ ounce peach brandy

Combine all the ingredients in a blender cup on High for 15 seconds. Add ¾ cup of ice (preferably crushed) and blend on High for 10 seconds. Pour into a cocktail glass. Garnish with the mint sprig.

(42) SKINNY DIP

2 ounces coconut water
1½ ounces blueberry vodka (such as Hangar One, Stoli, or Pearl)
1 ounce fresh lime juice
1 ounce sugar-free syrup (see page 15)
½ ounce cranberry juice
Lime wheel and maraschino cherry, for garnish

Combine all the ingredients in a cocktail shaker. Top with ice and shake moderately. Strain into a Collins glass filled with fresh ice. Garnish with the lime wheel and cherry.

← (43) PASSION FRUIT FEVER

I jalapeño slice, plus I for garnish
1½ ounces passion fruit vodka (such as SKYY)
I ounce simple syrup (see page 15)
½ ounce silver tequila
½ ounce fresh lime juice
½ ounce fresh lemon juice
Splash of fresh orange juice

Combine all the ingredients in a cocktail shaker. Top with ice and shake vigorously. Strain into a chilled cocktail glass. Garnish with a floating jalapeño slice.

(44) BEACHWALKER

1½ ounces 1800 Coconut Tequila
I ounce fresh orange juice
I ounce pineapple juice
½ ounce fresh lime juice
½ ounce simple syrup (see page 15)
Splash of grenadine (see page 13)
Maraschino cherry, for garnish

Combine all the ingredients in a cocktail shaker. Top with ice and shake vigorously. Strain into a Collins glass filled with fresh ice. Garnish with the cherry.

(45) AFTERNOON DELIGHT

Named after the 1970s song . . .

1 ounce simple syrup (see page 15)
1 ounce fresh orange juice
1 ounce pineapple juice
¾ ounce orange vodka
¾ ounce vanilla vodka
½ ounce spiced rum
½ ounce fresh lime juice
½ ounce heavy cream
Splash of club soda
Orange spiral twist, for garnish

Combine the simple syrup, orange juice, pineapple juice, vodkas, rum, lime juice, and cream in a blender cup. Add ¾ cup of crushed ice. Blend on High for 10 seconds. Add a splash of club soda. Pour into a tiki mug or cocktail glass. Garnish with the orange twist.

← (46) MANGO MADRAS

A tropical spin on the classic Madras made with a mango rum. Simple and delicious.

1½ ounces Cruzan mango rum
4 ounces fresh orange juice
1 ounce cranberry juice
Orange wheel, for garnish

Fill a Collins glass with fresh ice. Add the rum and orange juice. Top with the cranberry juice. Garnish with the orange wheel.

(47) PASSION & SPICE

2 ounces passion fruit juice
1¾ ounces Grand Marnier
½ ounce fresh lemon juice
½ ounce cinnamon spiced syrup (see page 15)
Cinnamon stick and orange wheel, for garnish

Combine all the ingredients in a cocktail shaker. Top with ice and shake vigorously. Strain into a chilled cocktail glass. Garnish with the cinnamon stick and a floating orange wheel.

(48) SPICED DAIQUIRI

2 ounces homemade spiced rum (recipe below)
I ounce fresh lime juice
I ounce simple syrup (see page 15)
Dash of bitters, optional (see page 11)
Vanilla bean sliver, for garnish

Combine all the ingredients in a cocktail shaker. Top with ice and shake vigorously. Strain into a chilled cocktail glass. Garnish with the vanilla bean sliver.

SPICED RUM

T his is a simple recipe to make your own spiced rum, which you can use in almost any spiced rum recipe. Feel free to add (or eliminate) any spices as you wish.

2 bottles (about 8 cups) of aged or amber rum*
2 vanilla beans (cut in half lengthwise, completely exposing the beans)
I cloved orange (poke about 5 to 6 cloves into a whole navel orange)
2 cinnamon sticks, broken into pieces
I whole nutmeg

Combine everything in an infusion jar. Keep in a cool, dark place. Let infuse for at least 2 days. Agitate ingredients. Taste. If you like what you taste, then strain out all the ingredients and bottle. If you want more spice, keep the infusion going for another day. Keep tasting and bottle it when you're ready.

*I recommend a rum that is relatively inexpensive and aged, but not a dark rum. You want a rum on the lighter side in order to pick up the many spices in the infusion. An aged rum that is rich and medium-bodied may not work as well. Some good choices would be Bacardi 8, Bacardi Gold, Cruzan Single Barrel Estate, Flor de Caña Seven Year, or 10 Cane.

(49) TAMURE COCKTAIL

A tamure (pronounced "Tah-MYUR-ee") is a Polynesian dance where the women shake their hips extremely fast, much like you should be shaking your cocktail. It was also the name of the sailboat my husband and I lived on in Marina Del Rey. It's a classic daiquiri shaken hard with any fruit you might have around in your fridge. Sometimes if we had a fruit salad left over from the night before, we would shake it in this cocktail.

> 4 ounces rum (white rum or amber rum is fine)
> 2 ounces fresh lime juice
> 2 ounces simple syrup (see page 15)
> ½ cup of any chopped fruit (watermelon, pineapple, honey-dew melon, mango, grapes, peaches, strawberries, etc.), plus more as desired for garnish

Combine all the ingredients in a cocktail shaker. Top with ice and shake vigorously. Strain into a cocktail glass. This can be served straight up (no ice) or on the rocks, whichever you prefer. Garnish with additional fruit.

(50) PINEAPPLE BLOSSOM
SANGRIA →

3 ounces sauvignon blanc
1 ounce agave nectar
1 ounce pineapple juice
¾ ounce Hangar One Mandarin Blossom vodka
½ ounce Cointreau
½ ounce fresh lemon juice
Splash of club soda
Pineapple ring, for garnish

Combine all the ingredients in a cocktail shaker. Top with ice and shake moderately. Strain into a Margarita glass or wine glass. Garnish with a floating pineapple ring.

(51) PAPAYA MAYA

1½ ounces aged rum
1 ounce fresh orange juice
¾ ounce orange Curaçao
½ ounce fresh lemon juice
½ ounce orange blossom honey
¼ cup papaya flesh
¼ cup fresh pineapple chunks, plus wedge for garnish
Orange wedge, for garnish

Combine all the ingredients in a blender cup. Blend on High for 10 to 15 seconds until smooth. Add 1 cup of ice and blend on High for another 10 to 15 seconds until smooth. Pour into a cocktail glass. Garnish with the pineapple and orange wedges.

← (52) FIREFLY

2 ounces fresh pineapple juice
1½ ounces Midori
1 ounce fresh lime juice
1 ounce simple syrup (see page 15)
¼ ounce absinthe

Combine all the ingredients in a cocktail shaker. Top with ice and shake hard for a good count to ten. Strain into a tall Collins glass filled with fresh ice. This drink has no garnish.

(53) YUZU GINGER MOJITO

I helped create this cocktail for P.F. Chang's, a pan-Asian restaurant chain. It's an Asian spin on a tropical classic.

10 mint leaves, plus sprig for garnish
1½ ounces Perfect Purée Yuzu Luxe Sour*
1 ounce sake
1 ounce TY-KU Citrus Liqueur (a soju infused with yuzu, honeydew, green tea, goji berry, and mangosteen)
1 ounce Ginger Beer (see page 26)

Combine the mint leaves, Perfect Purée Yuzu Luxe Sour, sake, and liqueur in a cocktail shaker. Top with ice and shake vigorously. Strain into a tall glass filled with fresh ice. Top with ginger beer and stir. Garnish with the mint sprig.

*Perfect Purée Yuzu Luxe Sour can be found at some Whole Foods Markets, other specialty grocers, or online (Amazon.com). If unable to find, combine 1 ounce of fresh lime juice, 1 ounce simple syrup, and 1 tablespoon yuzu marmalade or a few dashes of yuzu juice.

(54) THE HEATHEN CHILD →

Created by Tyson Buhler, a mixologist based in Phoenix, Arizona.

1 ripe strawberry, plus 3 slices for garnish
1½ ounces Domaine de Canton ginger liqueur
½ ounce Smith & Cross rum (or other Jamaican rum)
½ ounce fresh lime juice
½ ounce coconut cream (such as Coco Lopez)
¼ ounce Ramazotti (an Italian digestive)
1 dash Angostura bitters (see page 11)

In a mixing glass, muddle the strawberry. Add all the remaining ingredients. Top with ice and shake vigorously. Strain into a rocks glass filled with fresh crushed ice. Garnish with the 3 strawberry slices.

(55) KRACK OF DAWN

Made with a strong chilled coffee and Kraken, a spiced dark rum.

6 ounces chilled, strong (double-brewed) coffee
1 ounce Kraken spiced rum
1 ounce Patrón XO Cafe
1 ounce simple syrup (see page 15)
Splash of half-and-half

Combine all the ingredients in a blender cup. Add 2 to 3 cubes of ice and blend for 5 seconds. Pour into a tall Collins or highball glass filled with fresh ice. Serve with a straw.

← (56) OUTRIGGER

A rum sidecar.

Lemon wedge
Superfine sugar, for rim
1 ½ ounces aged rum
¾ ounce orange Curaçao
½ ounce fresh lemon juice

Wet the rim of a cocktail glass with the lemon wedge and dip the rim into a bowl of superfine sugar to coat. Set aside. Combine the rum, Curaçao, and lemon juice in a cocktail shaker. Top with ice and shake vigorously. Strain into the rimmed cocktail glass. This drink has no garnish.

(57) NO TAN LINES

Created by my friend and master mixologist Bridget Albert from Chicago, Illinois.

1 ounce Cruzan Black Cherry rum
1 ounce Cruzan Citrus rum
1 ounce double-brewed hibiscus tea
½ ounce fresh lemon juice
½ ounce agave nectar
2 ounces Mionetto Prosecco
Edible hibiscus flower, for garnish*

Fill a wine goblet with crushed ice and add the rums, tea, lemon juice, and agave nectar. Top with Prosecco and stir well. Garnish with the edible hibiscus flower.

*Edible hibiscus flowers can be found at Whole Food and other specialty grocers or online (www.wildhibiscus.com).

(58) JAMAICAN ME BLUE →

2 ounces white Jamaican rum (Appleton, Wray & Nephew, etc.)
1 ounce simple syrup (see page 15)
¾ ounce blue Curaçao
½ ounce fresh lime juice
½ ounce fresh lemon juice

Combine all the ingredients in a cocktail shaker. Top with ice and shake vigorously. Strain into a Collins glass or tiki glass filled with fresh ice. This drink has no garnish.

(59) SUMMER LEI

1½ ounces Hendrick's gin
1 ounce ruby red grapefruit juice
1 ounce fresh orange juice
1 ounce pineapple juice
½ ounce St. Germain Elderflower liqueur
½ ounce fresh lemon juice
½ ounce simple syrup (see page 15)
Splash of grenadine (see page 13)
Splash of 7-Up
Colored orchid or miniature lei, for garnish

Combine all the ingredients in a cocktail shaker. Top with ice and shake vigorously. Strain into a tall Collins glass filled with fresh ice. Garnish with the orchid or miniature lei.

(60) PINEAPPLE KIWI
COOLER

1 kiwi, peeled and cut into chunks
1½ ounces fresh pineapple juice
1 ounce Del Maguey VIDA mezcal
½ ounce Midori
½ ounce fresh lime juice
½ ounce simple syrup (see page 15)
Pineapple leaf, for garnish

Combine all the ingredients in a cocktail shaker. Top with ice and shake vigorously. Loosely strain into a Collins glass filled with fresh ice. (It's okay if seeds and some chunks of kiwi get into the glass.) Garnish with the pineapple leaf.

(61) PIÑA COLADA →

Created in San Juan, Puerto Rico, in the 1950s, this is a longstanding classic. While it can be made with a variety of rums—dark, aged, spiced, white, coconut—I like using a combination, but feel free to use whatever rums you like.

> 1½ ounces coconut cream (such as Coco Lopez)
> 1½ ounces pineapple juice
> 1 ounce aged rum
> 1 ounce coconut rum
> Splash of coconut milk (optional)
> Pineapple wedge, for garnish

Combine all the ingredients in a blender cup. Add 1 cup of ice. Blend on High until smooth. Pour contents into a tiki glass or tall glass. Garnish with the pineapple wedge.

(62) COCONUT WATER COLADA

This is a much lighter (lower-calorie) variation of the Piña Colada, and without the pineapple.

> 1 ounce white rum
> 1 ounce coconut milk
> 1 ounce simple syrup (see page 15)
> 1 ounce coconut water
> ½ ounce good, aged rum

Combine the white rum, coconut milk, simple syrup, and coconut water in a cocktail shaker. Top with ice and shake moderately. Strain into a bucket glass filled with fresh ice. Float the aged rum on top.

← (63) COCOA COLADA

2 ounces coconut cream
2 ounces pineapple juice
1½ ounces aged rum
½ ounce rich chocolate sauce, plus extra for the glass
Shredded coconut, for garnish

Combine all the ingredients in a blender cup. Add ¾ cup of ice and blend on High until smooth. Swirl some chocolate syrup in a tall glass. Pour the contents from the blender into the glass. Top with a sprinkle of shredded coconut.

(64) SPICED PLANTAIN COCKTAIL

1 ounce aged rum
1 ounce agricole rum (or 10 Cane rum)
1 ounce spiced plantain syrup (see page 15)
¾ ounce fresh lemon juice
1 egg white of a small egg (or ¾ ounce pasteurized egg white)
Dash of bitters (see page 11)

Combine the rums, syrup, lemon juice, and egg white in a cocktail shaker. Dry shake (without ice) for 5 to 10 seconds. Add ice and shake again for a good count to ten. Strain into a chilled cocktail glass. Top with a dash of bitters and swirl around.

(65) WHALE RIDER →

1 ½ ounces white rum
1 ounce coconut cream
1 ounce pineapple juice
½ ounce blue Curaçao
½ ounce fresh lime juice
½ ounce simple syrup (see page 15)
½ ounce overproof rum (float in lime half)

Squeezed out lime half, filled with an overproof rum, for garnish
Combine all the ingredients in a cocktail shaker. Top with ice and
shake vigorously. Strain into a large (wide-mouthed) glass filled with
fresh ice. Top with the squeezed-out lime half and fill with overproof rum. If feeling adventurous, light on fire.

(66) PASSION FRUIT VODKA GIMLET

2 ounces passion fruit vodka (such as SKYY)
1 ounce fresh lime juice
1 ounce simple syrup (see page 15)
Orange twist, for garnish

Combine all the ingredients in a cocktail shaker. Top with ice and
shake vigorously. Strain into a chilled cocktail glass. Garnish with
the orange twist.

(67) PINK FLAMINGO PUNCH

I created this cocktail as an LTO (Limited Time Only) for the Cheeseburger in Paradise restaurant chain.

I ounce **X-Rated Fusion Liqueur (passion fruit, blood orange, and mango liqueur, found at most liquor stores)**
I ounce **pineapple juice**
I ounce **cranberry juice**
½ ounce **fresh lime juice**
½ ounce **simple syrup (see page 15)**
½ ounce **Cabo Wabo reposado tequila**
½ ounce **Cruzan vanilla rum**
Splash of grenadine (see page 13)
Splash of 7-Up
Pink Flamingo, for garnish

Combine the liqueur, juices, simple syrup, tequila, rum, and grenadine in a cocktail shaker. Top with ice and shake vigorously. Strain into a large tiki glass. Top with a splash of 7-Up and stir. Garnish with the pink flamingo.

(68) KUMBAYA

1 ½ ounces rye whiskey
1 ounce Domaine de Canton ginger liqueur
1 ounce fresh orange juice
1 ounce pineapple juice
½ ounce fresh lemon juice
¼ ounce simple syrup (see page 15)
Piece of candied ginger, for garnish

Combine all the ingredients in a cocktail shaker. Top with ice and shake vigorously. Strain into a bucket glass filled with fresh ice. Garnish with the candied ginger.

(69) GREEN BAMBOO LATTE

2 ounces water
1 ½ ounces Zubrówka vodka*
1 ounce heavy cream
1 tablespoon green tea matcha powder
1 tablespoon sugar

Combine all the ingredients in a mixing glass. Stir until completely mixed. (Note: Depending on the brand and grade of matcha powder, adjust the amount of matcha powder and sugar, as needed.) Add ice and shake lightly. Strain into a tall Collins glass filled with fresh ice.

*Zubrówka vodka is infused with bison grass. It has a "sweet, aromatic grass" quality that works really well in this cocktail. You could also use a premium sake, such as TY-KU.

(70) SINGAPORE SLING

This classic Sling was created at the Raffles Hotel in Singapore.

2 ounces pineapple juice
1½ ounces gin (such as Tanqueray)
½ ounce Cherry Heering brandy
½ ounce Benedictine
½ ounce fresh lime juice
¼ ounce premium triple sec
¼ ounce grenadine (see page 13)
1 ounce club soda
Orange wheel and Maraschino cherry, for garnish

Combine the pineapple juice, gin, brandy, Benedictine, lime juice, triple sec, and grenadine in a cocktail shaker. Top with ice and shake vigorously. Strain into a tall Collins glass or tiki glass filled with fresh ice. Top with club soda and stir well. Garnish with the orange wheel and cherry.

(71) YELLOW BARRACUDA

1 ½ ounces gin (such as Hendrick's)
1 ½ ounces fresh pineapple juice
1 ounce limoncello
¾ ounce fresh lemon juice
¾ ounce simple syrup (see page 15)
½ ounce club soda

Combine the gin, pineapple juice, limoncello, lemon juice, and simple syrup in a cocktail shaker. Top with ice and shake vigorously. Add the club soda. Strain into a champagne coupe.

(72) SKINNY BUDDHA COSMO

This cocktail is made with Hangar One Buddha's Hand Citron vodka. Buddha's Hand (if you've never heard of it) is a pretty exotic and aromatic fruit often used by perfumers because of its potent citrus aromatics. It adds a lot of complexity to a cocktail. This is a low-calorie cocktail, hence the name Skinny Buddha.

> 4 lime wedges, plus 1 wheel for garnish
> 1 ounce Monin Sugar Free Unflavored Syrup (see page 15)
> 1½ ounces Hangar One Buddha's Hand Citron vodka
> 1 ounce cranberry juice

In a mixing glass, muddle the lime wedges with the sugar-free syrup. Add the vodka and cranberry juice. Top with ice and shake vigorously. Strain into a chilled cocktail glass. Garnish with a floating lime wheel.

(73) MIEHANA

A well-known new classic created by Jeff "Beachbum" Berry in 1999, who was tasked with creating a drink inspired by the orange groves in southern California. (Hint: Spell the drink name backward.)

> 1 ounce fresh lime juice
> 1 ounce fresh orange juice
> 1 ounce unsweetened pineapple juice
> 1 ounce Grand Marnier
> 1 ounce gold Puerto Rican rum
> 1 ounce coconut rum
> Orange wheel, ripe pineapple stick, and purple orchid, for garnish

Combine all the ingredients in a cocktail shaker. Top with ice and shake vigorously. Pour the contents into a tall glass or tiki mug. Garnish with the orange wheel, ripe pineapple stick, and a purple orchid, if available.

(74) PAINKILLER

The original was created at the Soggy Dollar Bar in the British Virgin Islands. It is similar to a piña colada, made with a dark rum (Pusser's Navy Rum), coconut cream, pineapple juice, orange juice, and grated nutmeg. There has been a little bit of a controversy over this iconic cocktail in recent years. The rum brand caused quite a stir in the cocktail community, after suing a well-known tiki bar in New York City (called Painkiller NY) over trademark infringement. They have since settled, but the bar had to legally change their name to PKNY.

4 ounces fresh pineapple juice
2 ounces dark rum (such as Pusser's Navy Rum)
1 ounce coconut cream
1 ounce fresh orange juice
Freshly grated nutmeg and pineapple stick, for garnish

Combine all the ingredients in a cocktail shaker. Top with ice and shake vigorously. Strain into a tall glass filled with fresh crushed ice. Top with grated nutmeg and a pineapple stick.

(75) SUFFERING BASTARD

Another great tiki classic, created by Joe Scialom at the Long Bar in Cairo, circa 1940s. This is a variation of the original.

I ounce gin
I ounce brandy
¾ ounce fresh lime juice
¾ ounce simple syrup (see page 15)
½ ounce triple sec
Dash of orange bitters
Top with ginger beer (see page 26)
Mint sprig, for garnish

Combine the gin, brandy, lime juice, simple syrup, triple sec, and bitters in a cocktail shaker. Top with ice and shake vigorously. Strain into a tall Collins glass filled with fresh ice. Top with ginger beer and stir. Garnish with the mint sprig.

(76) SUMMER SOLSTICE →

I ½ ounces Belvedere Pink Grapefruit vodka
I ounce ruby red pink grapefruit juice, strained
I ounce fresh orange juice
¾ ounce Aperol
½ ounce fresh lemon juice
½ ounce simple syrup (see page 15)
Pink grapefruit wheel, for garnish

Combine all the ingredients in a cocktail shaker. Top with ice and shake vigorously. Strain into a bucket glass filled with fresh ice. Garnish with the grapefruit wheel.

(77) CALIFORNIA
NEGRONI

 cross between a Gin and Tonic, Negroni, and a Greyhound. The perfect poolside summertime cocktail.

I ½ ounces gin
I ½ ounces ruby red grapefruit juice
¾ ounce Aperol
½ ounce fresh lime juice
½ ounce simple syrup (see page 15)
2 dashes Peychaud bitters (see page 11)
I ½ ounces tonic water
Pink grapefruit wheel and lime wheel, for garnish

Combine the gin, grapefruit juice, Aperol, lime juice, simple syrup, and bitters in a cocktail shaker. Top with ice and shake vigorously. Strain into a tall Collins glass filled with fresh ice. Top with tonic water and stir well. Garnish with the grapefruit and lime wheels.

← (78) PUERTO GONZO

Created by Martin Cate, owner and creator of Smuggler's Cove in San Francisco.

2 ounces Don Q Añejo rum
2 ounces coconut water
1 ounce guava soda (such as Bundaberg)
1 ounce club soda
¾ ounce fresh lime juice
½ ounce fleur de sel syrup (see page 12)
½ ounce Amontillado sherry
Mint sprig, for garnish

Combine all the ingredients in a blender cup. Add ¾ cup crushed ice. Blend for 8 to 10 seconds on High. Pour into a tall Collins (or Zombie) glass. Garnish with the mint sprig.

(79) R&R & RYE

A little rest, relaxation, and rye.

2 ounces rye whiskey
1 ounce fresh blood orange juice
¾ ounce fresh lemon juice
¾ ounce simple syrup (see page 15)
1 teaspoon grenadine (see page 13)
Dash of Angostura bitters (see page 11)
Egg white of 1 small egg (or ¾ ounce pasteurized egg white)
1 ripe blood orange wheel, for garnish

Combine all the ingredients in a cocktail shaker. Dry shake (without ice) for 10 seconds. (This will completely emulsify the egg white.) Add ice and shake for 10 seconds. Strain into a Collins glass filled with fresh ice. Garnish with the blood orange wheel.

(80) PINEAPPLE PISCO SOUR

2 ounces Pisco brandy (such as Encanto or Barsol)
1 ounce pineapple syrup (see page 15)
¾ ounce fresh lemon juice
1 egg white of small egg (or ¾ ounce pasteurized egg white)
Dash of Angostura bitters (see page 11)
Large piece of lemon peel, for garnish

Combine the brandy, pineapple syrup, lemon juice, and egg white in a cocktail shaker. Dry shake (without ice) for 10 seconds. (This will completely emulsify the egg white.) Add ice and shake vigorously for 10 seconds. Strain into a chilled cocktail glass. Top with a dash of bitters and swirl around with a toothpick. Garnish with the lemon peel.

(81) GREEN PARAKEET

1½ ounces citrus vodka
¾ ounce simple syrup (see page 15)
¾ ounce Midori
½ ounce fresh lemon juice
¼ ounce ginger juice
White orchid, for garnish

Combine all the ingredients in a cocktail shaker. Top with ice and shake *hard* for a good count to 10. Strain into a chilled cocktail glass. Garnish with the white orchid.

(82) BUFFALO MILK

Created at the Harbor Reef restaurant in Two Harbors, Catalina Island, off the coast of southern California. My husband and I drank many of these on our many sailing trips to Catalina Island. The drink is named after the wild buffalo that roam the island. They were left there by a film crew shooting a film in the 1920s.

1½ ounces half-and-half
1 ounce vodka
½ ounce dark crème de cocoa
½ ounce Kahlua
½ ounce crème de banana
Freshly grated nutmeg, for garnish

Combine all the ingredients in a blender cup. Top with ¾ cup of crushed ice. Blend for 10 seconds. Pour into a tall Collins glass. Garnish with grated nutmeg.

(83) TEST PILOT

A classic tiki drink created by Don the Beachcomber circa 1940s.

1½ ounces dark Jamaican rum
¾ ounce light rum
½ ounce fresh lime juice
½ ounce John D. Taylor's Velvet Falernum (see page 10)
3 teaspoon Cointreau
⅛ teaspoon Pernod pastis (or absinthe)
1 dash Angostura bitters (see page 11)
Maraschino cherry and lime wedge, for garnish

Combine all the ingredients in a blender cup. Add 1 cup of crushed ice and flash-blend for 5 to 10 seconds. Pour into a tiki mug or cocktail glass. Garnish with the cherry and lime wedge.

(84) BANANA HAMMOCK

¾ ounce Cruzan Black Strap rum
¾ ounce Cruzan light rum
½ ounce crème de banana
½ ounce dark crème de cocoa
I scoop vanilla ice cream
½ ripe banana, peeled
¼ cup cracked chocolate pieces or chocolate shavings, for garnish

Combine all the ingredients in a blender cup. Blend on High for 10 seconds. Add ¼ cup of ice and blend on High for another 10 seconds. Pour into a tiki mug or tall Collins glass. Top with the chocolate.

(85) HIBISCUS SWIZZLE →

1½ ounces gin
1 ounce simple syrup (see page 15)
1 ounce double-brewed hibiscus tea
½ ounce fresh lemon juice
Dash of orange bitters (see page 11)
White or purple orchid, for garnish

Combine all the ingredients in a tall Collins glass. Fill with crushed ice. Using a swizzle stick (see page 32), swizzle together until completely frosted and mixed. Garnish with the orchid.

(86) LEMONGRASS STIR

1½ ounces gin
1 ounce lemongrass syrup
½ ounce fresh lemon juice
Dash of lemon bitters (see page 13)
2 ounces Prosecco
Thin stalk of lemongrass
Lemon wheel, for garnish

Combine all the ingredients in a cocktail shaker. Top with ice and shake vigorously. Strain into a Collins glass filled with fresh ice. Top with Prosecco. Stir with the lemongrass. Garnish with the lemon wheel.

(87) MAI MANGO MOJITO

10 mint leaves
1 ounce fresh lime juice
½ ounce simple syrup (see page 15)
½ ounce orgeat syrup (see page 14)
1½ ounces Cruzan Mango rum
½ ounce gold or amber rum
3–4 1-inch mango chunks
Dash of orange bitters (see page 11)
Mint sprig and mango slice, for garnish

In a Collins glass, muddle the mint leaves with the lime juice, simple syrup, and orgeat. Add the rums, mango, and orange bitters. Top with crushed ice and stir well. Garnish with the mint sprig and mango slice.

(88) KEY LIME COCKTAIL →

1½ ounces vanilla vodka
¾ ounce key lime juice
¾ ounce simple syrup (see page 15)
½ ounce Midori, for color
Splash of cream
Splash of pineapple juice
Lime twist, for garnish

Combine all the ingredients in a cocktail shaker. Top with ice and shake vigorously. Strain into a chilled cocktail glass. Garnish with the lime twist.

(89) ISLAND SCREWDRIVER

5 ounces fresh orange juice
1½ ounces orange or mandarin vodka
1 ounce Passoã (passion fruit liqueur)
Lime wedge, for garnish

Combine all the ingredients in a cocktail shaker. Top with ice and roll contents. Pour directly into a tall Collins glass. Garnish with the lime wedge.

← (90) PEACH PIT

I whole ripe peach, peeled and cut into chunks
2 ounces fresh orange juice
1½ ounces peach vodka (such as Ciroc)
¾ ounce Amaretto di Saronno
Agave nectar (optional)

Combine the peach chunks, orange juice, vodka, and amaretto in a blender cup. Blend on High until smooth. Add ¾ cup of ice and blend on High again until smooth. Add agave nectar for additional sweetness, if needed.

(91) YELLOW PARROT

¼ cup pineapple chunks
I ounce simple syrup (see page 15)
I ounce fresh lime juice
1½ ounces white rum
½ ounce John D. Taylor's Velvet Falernum (see page 10)
2 dashes bitters (see page xxx)
Mint sprig and pineapple stick, for garnish

In a Collins glass, muddle the pineapple with the simple syrup and lime juice. Add the white rum, Velvet Falernum, and bitters. Top with crushed ice and stir well. Garnish with the mint sprig and pineapple stick.

(92) SUMMER WIND →

10 ripe blueberries, plus extra for garnish
2 ripe strawberries, plus 1 strawberry half for garnish
1½ ounces fresh orange juice
1½ ounces pineapple juice
1½ ounces Jamaican rum
1 ounce coconut cream (such as Coco Lopez)
Pineapple leaf, for garnish

Combine all the ingredients in a blender cup. Blend on High for 10 seconds. Add ¾ cup of ice. Blend on High for 10 to 15 seconds until smooth. Pour into a tropical cocktail glass. Garnish with the pineapple leaf, strawberry half, and a few blueberries.

(93) MACADAMIA NUT CHI CHI

Another tiki classic circa 1960s, adapted by Jeff "Beach-bum" Berry. A Chi Chi is a Piña Colada made with vodka instead of rum. This one also includes a macadamia nut liqueur. If you can't find this at your local liquor store, try using a walnut liqueur (Nux Alpina or Nocello). Frangelico (a hazelnut liqueur) would also work.

8 ounces unsweetened pineapple juice
4 ounces vodka (try a creamy potato vodka, such as Chopin)
2½ ounces macadamia nut liqueur
2 ounces coconut cream (such as Coco Lopez)

Combine all the ingredients in a blender cup. Add 2 cups of ice. Blend on High until smooth. (This cocktail should be fairly thick.) Pour into tiki mugs or cocktail glasses.

← (94) HONEY HIDALGO

2 ounces reposado or añejo tequila
1 ounce fresh orange juice
¾ ounce fresh lemon juice
½ ounce honey
Orange twist, for garnish

Combine all the ingredients in a blender cup with 2 to 3 cubes of ice. Blend for 5 to 6 seconds on High. Pour into a large champagne coupe glass. Garnish with the orange twist.

(95) MOBY DICK

 large-format punch that is meant to serve many.

Peel of 3 lemons
3 teaspoons white sugar
16 ounces orange vodka
6 ounces fresh lemon juice
6 ounces grenadine (see page 13)
2 ounces fresh orange juice
2 ounces Grand Marnier
½ ounce orange bitters (see page 11)
16 ounces club soda

In a large punch bowl, muddle the lemon peels with the sugar. (This will extract the oil from the skins and mix it with the sugar. This is also called an oleo saccharum, or oil sugar.) Add the vodka, lemon juice, grenadine, orange juice, Grand Marnier, and bitters. Add lots of ice (about 10 cups). Add the club soda, stir, and serve by ladling into punch cups.

MAKES 8 SERVINGS

(96) KAMA SUTRA →

4 ounces guava nectar
4 ounces pineapple juice
2 ounces coconut rum
2 ounces vanilla vodka
2 ounces spiced rum
2 ounces premium triple sec (orange liqueur)
2 ounces fresh lime juice
2 ounces simple syrup (see page 15)

Combine all the ingredients in a blender cup. Add 2 cups of ice. Blend on High until smooth, about 10 seconds. Pour into a tiki bowl. Serve with straws.

MAKES 3 SERVINGS

(97) SCORPION BOWL

n adaptation of a classic tiki punch, served family-style. Originally created circa 1950s by Trader Vic.

4 ounces white rum
4 ounces fresh lemon juice
2 ounces orange Curaçao
1½ ounces orgeat syrup (see page 14)
1 ounce apricot brandy
6 ounces fresh orange juice
Float of overproof rum (optional)

Combine the white rum, lemon juice, Curaçao, orgeat syrup, brandy, and orange juice in a blender cup. Add 2 scoops of ice. Blend on High for 10 seconds. Pour into a tiki bowl. Add more ice to the tiki bowl. Float the overproof rum on top, if desired. If feeling adventurous, light on fire. Serve with several long straws.

MAKES 6–8 SERVINGS

(98) UPSIDE DOWN PINEAPPLE CAKE

2 tablespoons crushed pineapple
1 ounce coconut cream (such as Coco Lopez)
1 ounce pineapple juice
¾ ounce coconut vodka or rum (such as SKYY Coconut or Cruzan Coconut)
¾ ounce Frangelico
Lemon wedge
Dollop of whipped cream
Small pineapple wedge, for garnish

In a large martini glass, add the crushed pineapple and set aside. In a cocktail shaker, combine the coconut cream, pineapple juice, coconut vodka or rum, and Frangelico. Squeeze the juice from a lemon wedge into the shaker and discard the wedge. Top with ice and shake vigorously. Strain over the crushed pineapple. Top with a dollop of whipped cream and garnish with the pineapple wedge.

(99) HOT PINEAPPLE TODDY

I whole pineapple, cored, peeled, and cut into 1-inch chunks
(or buy precut chunks), plus 6–8 pineapple sticks for garnish
64 ounces apple cider
I teaspoon ground cinnamon
6 whole cloves
375 ml bottle spiced rum, plus more if needed

Prepare the pineapple, peeling and cutting into cubes. Add the flesh and juice from the cutting board to a saucepan. Add the apple cider, cinnamon, and cloves and heat on High. Bring to a boil. Lower heat and cook for 10 minutes. Keep on low heat until ready to serve. (This can also be heated in a crockpot on low heat, but it may take up to 45 minutes to be ready.) Preheat the mugs by filling with very hot water; let sit for 1 minute. Discard the water and ladle the pineapple cider into the mugs. Add 1 to 1½ ounces of the spiced rum. Garnish with the pineapple stick.

MAKES 6–8 SERVINGS

(100) HOT BUTTERED RUM

One of my most favorite holiday cocktails. I like making this in a blender (versus making the batter the night before); it's faster and I like the texture a little better. It's hot and "fluffy."

I stick butter, unsalted, softened
2 cups light brown sugar
8 ounces of rum (can also use a spiced rum)
I ounce mezcal
I teaspoon vanilla extract
I teaspoon ground cinnamon
½ teaspoon grated nutmeg
Pinch of allspice
Pinch of mace (optional)

Heat a kettle of water. Preheat coffee mugs with hot water from the faucet and let sit. Meanwhile, add all the ingredients to a blender cup. Blend on High for 45 seconds to 1 minute. The ingredients will actually start to heat up in the blender cup. Once the water in the kettle comes to a boil, turn the blender to its very lowest setting and *slowly* add the hot water. Keep adding until the blender cup is almost full. Discard the hot water in the mugs. Turn off the blender and pour the mixture into the mugs.

MAKES 4–5 SERVINGS

(101) HOT BUTTERED BANANA

Same recipe as above, but add ¼ cup of crème de banana liqueur and 2 ripe peeled bananas.

INDEX

A

Afternoon Delight, 66
Aperol About It, 33

B

Bahama Mama. 25
Banana Daiquiri, 43
Banana Hammock, 109
Beachbum's Own, 57
Beachwalker, 65
Blackberry Pineapple Sidecar, 46
Black Pepper Mandarin Margarita, 54
Blue Hawaiian, 20
Buffalo Milk, 106

C

California Negron, 100
Caribbean Cosmopolitan, 26
Classic Daiquiri, 43
Cocoa Colada, 87
Coconut Water Colada, 84
Corona-Rita, 56

D

Dark & Stormy, 27
Demerara Dry Float, 31
Dragon's Breath, 59

E

El Diablo, 28
Eureka Punch, 35

F

Firefly, 75
Fog Cutter, 40

G

Ginger Beer (non-alcoholic), 26
Green Bamboo Latte, 92
Green Parakeet, 106
Grilled Pineapple Margarita, 53
Guava Basil Cooler, 36

H

Heathen Child, The, 76
Hemingway Daiquiri, 44
Hibiscus Swizzle, 110
Honey Hidalgo, 121

Hot Buttered Rum, 127
Hot Buttered Banana, 127
Hot Pineapple Toddy, 126
Hurricane, 32

I

Island Screwdriver, 114

J

Jamaican Me Blue, 80

K

Kama Sutra, 122
Key Lime Cocktail, 114
Kingston Club, The, 60
Krack of Dawn, 76
Kumbaya, 92

L

Lemongrass Stir, 110
Lime in da Coconut, 61

M

Macadamia Nut Chi Chi, 118
Mai Mango Mojito, 113
Mainsail, 60
Mai Tai, 16
Major Bailey, 28
Mango Madras, 69
Mango Mai Tai, 39
Miehana, 86
Missionary's Downfall, 62
Moby Dick, 121
Morning Dew Sparkle, 40
Mosquito Bite, 57

N

No Tan Lines, 79

O

Outrigger, 79

P

Painkiller, 97
Papaya Maya, 72
Passion Fruit Fever, 65
Passion Fruit Vodka Gimlet, 88
Passion & Spice, 69
Peach Pit, 117
Pegu Club Cocktail, 51
Piña Colada, 84
Pineapple Blossom Sangria, 72

Pineapple Kiwi Cooler, 81
Pineapple Needle, 45
Pineapple Pisco Sour, 104
Pink Flamingo Punch, 91
Planter's Punch, 19
Puerto Gonzo, 103

Q

Queens Park Swizzle, 61

R

R & R & Rye, 103
Rum Runner, 23
Rum Swizzle, 32

S

Scorpion Bowl, 122
Sidewinder's Fang, 22
Singapore Sling, 93
Skinny Buddha Cosmo, 96
Skinny Dip, 62
Spiced Daiquiri, 70
Spiced Plantain Cocktail, 87
Spiced Rum Daiquiri, 70
Suffering Bastard, 99
Summer Lei, 80
Summer Solstice, 100
Summer Wind, 118
Sunburn, 48

T

Tamure Cocktail, 71
Test Pilot, 107
Tropical Itch, 49
Tropical Margarita, 56

U

Upside Down Pineapple Cake, 125

W

Whale Rider, 88

Y

Yellow Barracuda, 94
Yellow Parrot, 117
Yuzu Ginger Mojito, 75

Z

Zombie, 30